Blame Yours

Philip Miller

Published by Nine Pens Press
2024
www.ninepens.co.uk

ISBN: 978-1-917150-05-7
025

For my father, Christopher Miller (1936-99)

Withershins

By this light, the fault line is red,
as if gnawed,
a maw of bleeding rock
open, a broken jaw

loose over the rusting dale
turning slowly in the autumn.
Silence sluices the cold gill
in webs of grey water light

while Simon Sorcerer, converted fool,
gives up his magick
to follow the invisible man,
anticlockwise to the winter sun.

Count the beasts
in the lost words, the wizard said.
We can count them true,
under the shadow of the fault:

Yan – once loved,
Tan – all lost,
Tetherer – whatever I was,
Petherer – I am no longer.

In the churchyard, under
the square tower, in the
cold rich rain,
the vampire is fixed

to a long unlife by an iron pin.
Old Hodgson, a long black insect:
grinning still, dog blood on his lips,
wet necked, a foot inside holy ground.

You, friend, can abandon your magick
under the blessed fell, dripping with light,
by the lime kiln's mossy roof,
a bath for green children.

Sorcerer, parched by the dry falls,
why give up spells that manifest
for a word, the rumour of a great man,
already dead, alive, and gone again?

But hope on, and lay down the old spells.
It is an old church do, a traditional rite,
for the lush green lady, changing hexes
for crosses, warming dead blood

in her warm stockinged thigh.
Laid heavy soft, after the wedding,
hungover, so warm, so warm over my
body, not daring to move.

Oh, this old harmony,
congruent to the drone
of the unrevealed threnody
in the drip, drip, drip in the bowl –

(it takes a brave man
to wear such white, clean trousers
past the age
of forty)

tumbling from the first floor window
past the luscious plum tree, into the Dee's
fossil beach, where dead white years
are millions embedded, minute galaxies,

older than a forgotten kiss
on the grains of the university steps.
These lips dead, peeled, and grown again
on the ragged mouth of the headland

between the limestone and the Silurian,
a life of cracks and falls and abrasions,
subversions, diversions, seen and unseen
like the whispering foam of the flowing river

or the tap, tap, tap of the typewriter
my father left,
his novel half done -
not novel, and not finished -

but still written, inside stories
anecdotes, books, the tiresome subsequent lies,
like the eyes that nose the barbed wire:
contained, stinking, uncounted, unnamed.

Simon the Sorcerer, sick, gone now, roving by the plague
village, a rumour under trees.
The hearths grassed over,
their paths grassed over, in the trees –

and this pinioned vampire,
undead, grins asleep and awake,
alone of all his kind in the dale,
A life half lived, and half over.

See –

stock snuffle over the plot
where we will eventually lie.
We've stopped saying Hi
and begun to say Goodbye.

Yan, tan, tetherer, petherer,
We can count them over, 'til sleep.
The following all gone,
the worthy spells all gone.

Hush, now, wheesht,
we sleep soon, sorcerer, we soon sleep.
You need much memory to tell such lies,
soft weak fossil, curled against the fault line.

Note:
In Dent, Cumbria, a vampire is said to be buried in the churchyard.

Sons

In the fragile sleepless night,
I lift his breathing body to its rest.
Folded like a shotgun
across my weeping arms and breast.

I lay beside him as he lies,
knowing one day he'll see me dead.
And all my dreams of flying,
were my father carrying me to bed.

Cold promise

Spring returns, green
with its annual lies.
Like diseased sheep,
runners circle the park.

Is what we take for hope,
only a fresh reiteration
of the orbit's annual theme,
the rest a recurring dream.

On the mud track home,
the antic birds build nests:
the shreds of former trees,
bindings, moss and leaves,

recollections of past safety,
bound for the future young.
The woven centre of absence
is a cold promise, like the crown

that bled when it was worn,
and a song the birds also know,
that their busy, sewing silence,
is the work and patience of love.

Ledes I- III

I

She was wheezing, and the kid was in pain.
'Upstairs', she said, and so clattering we went,
the snapper cracking his long lens on the thin walls.
In the boy's pale room, the black mould prayed.

'The Lady', she said, pointing, and we made notes
and took pics. The red boy and his nebulizer hissed,
like the midden outside. 'Clear as day,' she said, pointing
to the Mother of Christ, reborn in spores, praying
for an end to the spreading damp, the disease, the rain.

II

Flat 44 at the high rise, and we were up for the death knock.
Shouting through a slit of light at the wretched mother.
How did she feel about her boy, Colin? Killed in a wreck that
night. The lift was broken, and the stairwell dank. Black clouds
shook with sudden rain, and from the height the light stopped,
blocked.

The smudged distance hovered. I waited, and watched the door,
but did not rap again, or make her talk. Back in the gauzy office,
we shrugged and carried on. 'Nowt there,' I lied, and they
dropped him to page nineteen, a hamper beneath a car ad.

III

To a place of hypnotism, for a feature on past-life regression.
After a count, I was gone. To a black trench, sick with slaughter,
screaming at stumps gouting into mud. I spooled back in time
and saw a diseased man, looking over winnowed fields,
pockmarked and alone, a splintered spire on the plain.

Time as mesh, and each string a line to be cut, or edited.
Time as text, and each moment erasable as ink, like blood
sponged from a stump. I cried out, and began to bang my head.
He woke me, and passed a tissue. 'Lots of colour,' they said.
Words dripped slow. I typed with his hands, gripping my left leg.

A leaf

Light as light,
the ghost of a tree aflame,
the fire etched in flat tin, waiting

for warmth to move into the silent woods.
Muddy track scabbed with dead leaves,
remnants, nest jetsam, and the silence

broken in high branches by birds fortifying, calling.
By the path there is only wood: copied, pasted,
ditches dead with choking, gates broken,

and a stilled stream, strangled by windfall.
Are you here? In the sudden glare of the sun,
between track and sky, in these insistent feet

moving forward from the ruin to the river.
Are you silently here. In mud, and forest,
and the supernova.

Happy Birthday

I am the beast to be rendered.
Put coins in my ears,
scald my flesh,
and scrape off these old bristles.
Quick! – pull hard the hot guts, flush them
for sausages,

the boys can play with the bladder,
once it has dried in the sun.
Butch my arse,
thighs, trotters and haunch,
and chuck my eyes to the cats,
for sport.

Find use for this tongue's meat,
and darling: the parts you tasted, taste better
fried.
Give spare ribs to the neighbours,
and my room to the piglets in winter.
Use every part of me, except my
cries.

Ledes (Montmartre)

I
He meant to bang his head off the wall,
But it was hessian, matting and gall.

He looked for knives.
But she had hidden them all
and the kettle would not boil,
So went into the yellow air of the mall.

Dildos were racked in the sex shop like clubs.
In the church he spent 100 Euros on candles,
and dropped his kebab in the tramp's satchel.

II
The city is not asleep.
Orange haze, men huddled, and lights weeping
between trees, befuddled doorways, the ochre air.

In the inundations, they once carried each other there -
through flooded boulevards, man on man, tethered.
At Rue San Dominique a crowd of washed faces gathered.

In the cork lies baffled constellations.
At the cash point, a soft-faced cutpurse –
one hand behind his back – gave instructions to deceive, and ran,
then dropped to the tiles and slept, or worse.

And the funicular is steadfast, stuck
on the ascent to the Sacre-Coeur.

Serrano and Manchego

Your favourite café has closed down, I saw today,
passing by on the bus, the flashing windows white
with paint, the sale sign up, and inside the spray
of dust on tables where we sat and ate that time

when you said, smiling, there was little more
that could be done. Strange drugs, a new diet,
surgery maybe. It was the good of goodbye,
cast back always in ever forward time.

Taking my hand you said don't be sorry, be happy,
and your veins were blue and rich in that sunshine.
Every time something happens,
it happens for the last time.

Dismantling the cot

The thread turns, gold lines twisting, as the hand curls,
the fastenings slip out in a steady brass coil and the joints loosen
with a shake, the cot slips in the hand, the screw unfurls
and it all comes apart – the bed cracked, in five weak pieces on the floor.

Your first, and the last we will have to unscrew,
no need for slats and bars now, and this tiny pale cage
becomes new doors laid on the wall, with metal slewing
in a jar for another father who will reach in and shush.

The thread turns, time passes with each turn and roll,
the fastenings slip and the threads are loosened and parted.
Now in the night, no cries or calls for help, no tiny upturned palms,
just footsteps, a life of yearning, and the search for warmth in the dark.

Memorial

In the hospital lift,
stuck with an empty wheelchair,
a food trolley, an exhausted nurse,
and it fails, and we are stuck.

My father waits dying elsewhere.
A button is hammered like a nail,
and we are all cross,
waiting for the metal ropes to pull,

us out of this dank room to another,
where there is more space
but less hope, and electric light
illuminates nothing worth seeing.

The lift is stuck in Darlington Memorial.
The nurse sleeps in the wheelchair,
we eat the last chips, and someone
produces cards, and we all say Snap.

Panic in Haymarket

All night in the wrong bed,
still reeling from no sleep
and the ecstasy,

interviewing the man
from the Arts Council
and me green and sweaty

and he asked me if I was OK,
and I said: Yes, it's just a bit of flu.
Brimful eyes still heartful of you.

And after, vomiting in St Mary's,
three spires and a chaser
in the pub by the train station,

I texted the wrong person
about the wrong thing
and the tracks seemed inviting

for a moment of terror,
split by guilt and keening
desire, that Holy hunger,

for you, as if for the first time.
Heaven, never again, the body
becomes inured to that pain.

On the train home, thinking of lies,
sweating, and my weak flannel.
Turning myself into an animal.

Christmas

There was that day I ate a bauble.
Sheen like kelp, it was glassy and long.
Plucked from the tree, its silver strobed,
as light as my arm.

A bite and the frail mollusc was undone.
The glimmering splinters
were scales glinting
in soft red gum and tongue.

The sleepy room roused in dozy panic:
to the boy crying through broken glass,
the mouth a slush of flickering blood.
The jags were picked out, like nits.

Christmas, with bleeding.
And the ghost in the spare room, rousing
the cat to kill its kittens, an empty chair
at the table, and stardust glitter in the teeth.

Like love

In the high hills in the unforgotten dale a stream still runs.
One night after our row, I fell up the stairs in the dark close,
and my brow juddered, and the blood from my sharp heart
came sudden like this memory. My fingers wet, we rose
to the high hills again, and time bent around my head.

The stream runs still, not ceasing or waiting, and joins
another river now, rising from its beck, but still to the sea,
the same sea. It is still rising, undimmed and silently mine,
asleep or with music, and like the stream that always runs,
whether seen or not, touched or not, it is, like love, outside time.

Doleron

We were all going to the beach,
but the boys were sleeping,
and what did it really matter -

so I went alone towards the immensity,
and at the cabin there was café but no lait,
but that was fine, and I sat on the rise

with the people standing at the sea,
on the lids of the eye of the world,
staring at the flesh turning colours

and the waves turning over themselves
smiling over the hidden reef, salty mist
and spume, the teeth of the high tide.

The coffee, spare and black, and the past
funneling between the rocks of my ears
and the horizon a guillotine cutting across

it all. The boat you took age six from there
to here, your mother searching at the quay
for all the loss she could not see.

This tide envelops that same tide.
Look at the woman over there, head over body.
And you in hospital crying, like that child,

holding your hand, with nothing to be done.
And the waves here closing over the shelf
of shame, at the past which still breaks

on the present, eroding it all to this sand,
arming the waters around this grey coracle:
whispering over again, hissing against the land -

Blame yourself. Blame yourself.
Blame yourself. Oh Lord, Oh God: I blame myself.

New Music

Across the morning wall,
a geometric fall of light –
shadows from the tilted blind
paint fresh staves and score,

dust motes hang as notes
on the shimmering sheet.
Below, the still wet towel hangs
soundless like a hood

or an overture, an offering,
another field for sound.
Caught in this volume of silence
and light, dumb with suffering,

the tender lucent script
slowly dissolves into itself, and
was never there: a plan
unfollowed, a song unsung.

In memory

He was to the side, and rarely in mind.
But now he is dead. There was loose hair,

a wet mouth, struggling in class. But nothing there
for years: weak memories of a frail single child

who may have been a friend. Someone pale, wild
and unhappy. Something raw and too sore to share

in his glossy stare, clumsiness of pose, the lack of care
in his clothes, his blare and cough, his untidy mind.

Now, you say: 'Well, he drank himself to death.'
But who knows now what he tried to drown –

absent love, love gone wrong, or something worse
than love. He broke up the glasses,

and naked threw his lean body clean through.
You say: 'He was never really happy.'

But no. There was green summer grass,
light on water, and a boy, funny and shy.
A child outside of his laughter.

Breakage

The weight of the snow overwhelmed the panes
and the old skylight crashed into the bathroom

in a sudden short shout of bomb noise and breakage.
A heap of snow and glass, dirt and a shattered nest

from the roof, left by the gulls for another winter,
was now furious wreckage in the tangled tub.

We let the snow melt, and glass slide to the drain,
amid twigs and roof moss, chimney clay, sea shells.

In the silt: speckled unborn eggs from the past summer,
buttons, glinting things, golf balls, soft brown feathers.

We covered the hole with board and waited for respite
from the snow, and the wind, these violent intruders

that brought blood, calamity, splintered blades,
and this strange broken home, falling into ours.

Deepdale
(i)

Dream eyelash
caught in the eye,

mote streams beams
in day sleep and night.

The tip of a finger
cannot find or fix you.

Sliding daydream hair,
splintering sight,

sleep inside
the untouchable sliver.

(ii)

Driving, not moving,
in silence,

heart split by my own lack,
and grim hills

stack in stilled waves.

But then the air blooms,
and the valley opens -

we glide into the soft golden lake,
gleaming in a world that can never be.

Weight becomes light, momentarily.

A luminous sheet had been laid over the deep dale,
and breath becomes a passing prayer.

The side of life

The mould in the shower
hangs, a speckled negative
of a long dead galaxy
and in the grey garden
the earth is sandy
where we shook the ashes.

Later, in the big tent
the old grave poet
says poetry should be
on the side of life.
But every cold night,
when light has melted

dry dread appears again,
spare and plain,
and despite the rhyming
and the goodwill
and the wishing -
nothing can matter.

Yet a lingering ghost
of my old unsafe love,
whispers that at least
the falling and rising
between this deep
and any lesser pain
is a form of flight,
and a movement.

Weight

They are heavier now, soft legs melting lead
over my arms, and we move them from our bed
to theirs. Eyes move under pale lids, sight
blind to the strand that lights their coming years.

It's not often you carry the most precious thing:
there is no weight to music, to forgiveness, or to love.
In time this stress will move from our arms to theirs -
to be carried by them, and be all that they can bear.

Unsent

The old words lie
on the cold screen
like the ice in the window
where the fish are laid.

Loss, anger, lust, anomie
recollected in futility:
that drama's run is ended
but the script remain complete

and words still act and talk
even if their prompt is silenced.
So who remembers the party
where I was a neanderthal,

and did you ever really
take a hammer to your arm
or burn my eye with a cigarette.
Here: you asked for forgiveness

and I never replied -
an answer lies in draft, unsent.
If such words are never read,
are they ever really meant.

Fox

The fox returned.
Slipping between, brushy
in the lane, slight as a
lean comma, eyes aglint
like wounds and liquid.

A stench, a grave scent,
and life: rough claws,
silent, revenant paws
and still, barely pausing
black in the street light.

Red under the still moon,
a ribbon of movement.
I knew it was you, watching,
returning in baffled form.
Your bed not yet changed,

stains stitched into the quilt.
Now at night often bins rattle
with no wind, the morning guilt
met with scat, scattered scraps,
an upturned heart. A yell.

Little Newsham

The hammer sets the rhythm
of the footsteps on the path
to the door of the old house

at the end of the old village.
The pear tree by the window
is long gone, all sawn down

for better television reception,
and the attic is drunk with ghosts
of mine and other bodies

hanging from the bridge
by the flaming hollow tree
in the glare of the lightning

storm, rattling a glockenspiel
clack from the skeletal woods
shivering with undead clamour.

The blacksmith's hammer
beating white metal to red and black
and the children, ravenous, running

through the shadows between leaves,
a whispering black archipelago.
The drenching wave is cast

dowsing the red flowers,
watched by the owls who murmur:
you can drown in an inch of water.

And in the Big House
where the big wet men stood,
the Tudor wood is soft

with mould, and faceless
eyes fleet as swallows
swim in the porous red walls.

Black taped eyes lull in the pond,
and under the spare enamel bath
a sliding grey pile of pornography.

Please, close them all, and return.
For here, like dreams,
we are without time.

As the blacksmith beats
flowers, wet like metal
from red fire to rhyme

with toys that stand eyeless,
coated in the skin of dust
of abandonment, and of lust

sealed in the cooling metal.
See the remorseless move
from dust to mud to earth

while the seasons grind the ever mill.
Buried where the pear tree stood
is a book, a poem, a rhyme,

and hands pinned by iron flowers.
Time beaten, time stilled, time
driven outside of its beating power.

Love Song

Every night, like a vet,
I put the house to sleep,
check the children
are still dreaming
and lock the cats
in the kitchen so
at the Devil's hour
they do not bite my head.

In the dark, the mind shakes.
Maybe despite death, the grave
is like this: deep and dread
and still drenched in fear,
alive to the next dead day,
the endless years to come.
But under my thin pillow,
I feel your fingers, and find them.

The grave is for one,
but our bed is for two,
and that answerless pain
can be numbed till tomorrow.
Our hands and fears entwine
and once joined, disappear.
Like tears that flow together,
pool, and become our mirror.

Acknowledgments:

I would like to gratefully thank One Hand Clapping, The North, Gutter Magazine, Birmingham Poetry Literary Journal, Eyelash, Poet's Directory, Structo and The Madrigal for publishing poems which are included here. I would also like to thank my family and friends, for their forbearance.